Reindeer

Size: 11½" x 14" [29.2cm x 35.6cm]
Skill Level: Average

Materials

- ❑ Three sheets of 7-mesh plastic canvas
- ❑ Two 8mm brown eyes
- ❑ Five 12mm jingle bells
- ❑ Craft glue or glue gun
- ❑ Worsted-weight or plastic canvas yarn; for amounts see Color Key.

NOTE

- Graphs continued on pages 2–4.

Stitching Step By Step

1 Cut and work pieces according to graphs.

2 With matching colors as shown in photo on back cover, whipstitch A pieces wrong sides together; repeat with B pieces. For Arms (make 2), whipstitch two corresponding C pieces wrong sides together. For Legs (make 2), whipstitch one D No. 1 and one D No. 2 wrong sides together.

3 Matching same-colored ◆s, with matching colors, tack pieces together as indicated. Glue eyes to Head Front as indicated. Hang or display as desired.

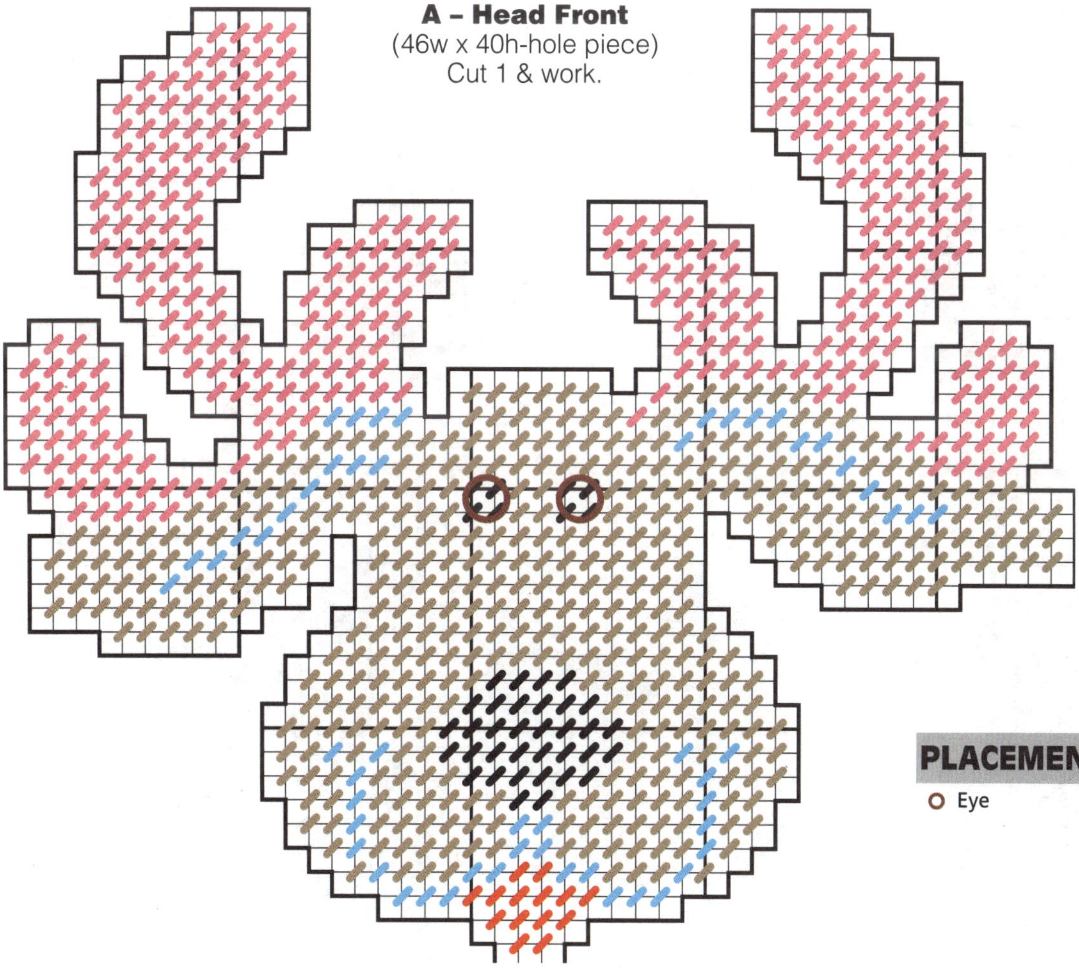

COLOR KEY
Reindeer

WORSTED-WEIGHT

	Tan	40 yds. [36.6m]
	Red	40 yds. [36.6m]
	Green	20 yds. [18.3m]
	Dk. Brown	15 yds. [13.7m]
	Black	12 yds. [11m]
	Dk. Gray	2 yds. [1.8m]
	Med. Brown	2 yds. [1.8m]

A – Head Front
(46w x 40h-hole piece)
Cut 1 & work.

PLACEMENT KEY

O Eye

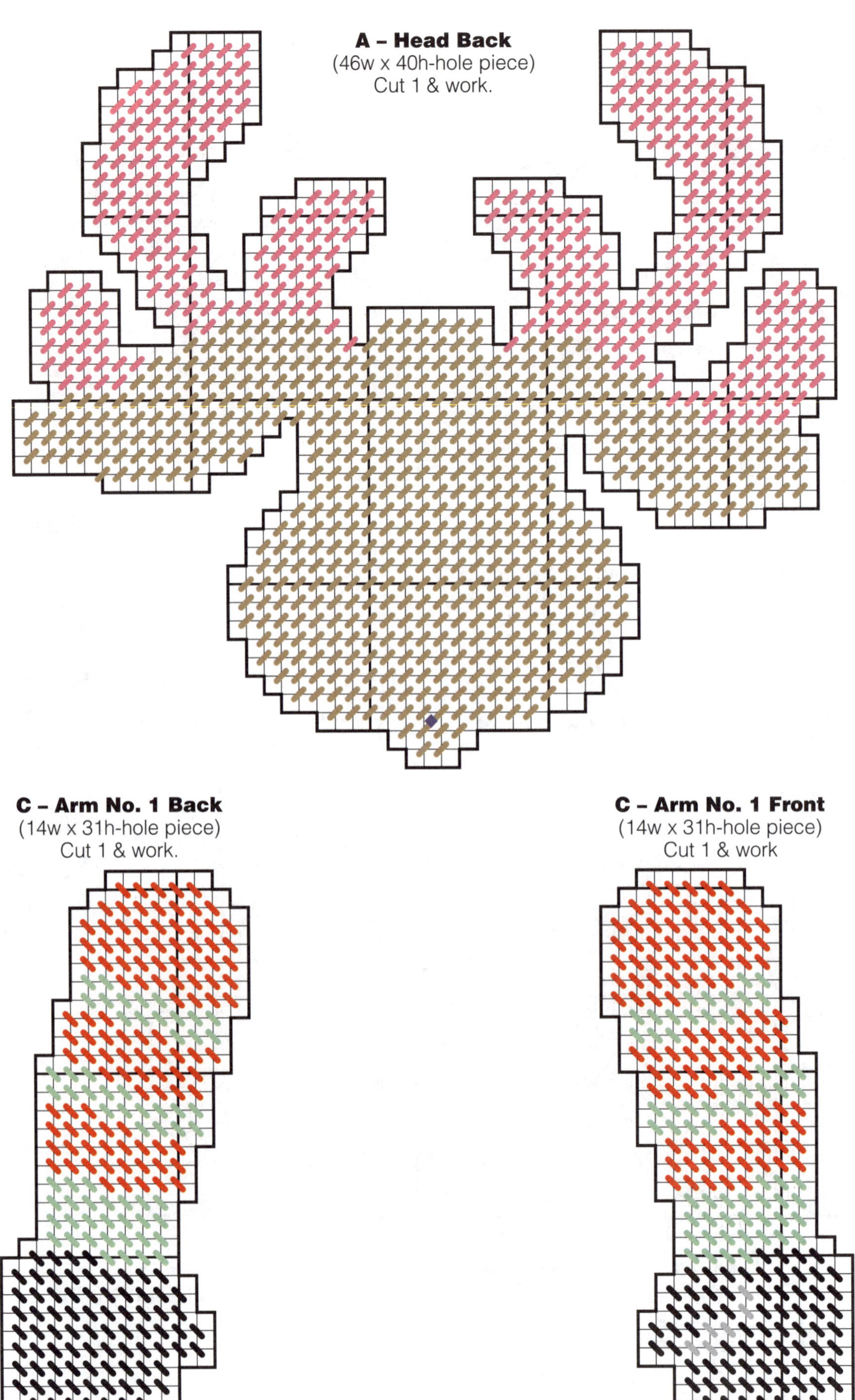

A – Head Back
(46w x 40h-hole piece)
Cut 1 & work.
C – Arm No. 1 Back
(14w x 31h-hole piece)
Cut 1 & work.
C – Arm No. 1 Front
(14w x 31h-hole piece)
Cut 1 & work

COLOR KEY
Reindeer

WORSTED-
WEIGHT

Tan
40 yds. [36.6m]

Red
40 yds. [36.6m]

Green
20 yds. [18.3m]

Dk. Brown
15 yds. [13.7m]

Black
12 yds. [11m]

Dk. Gray
2 yds. [1.8m]

Med. Brown
2 yds. [1.8m]

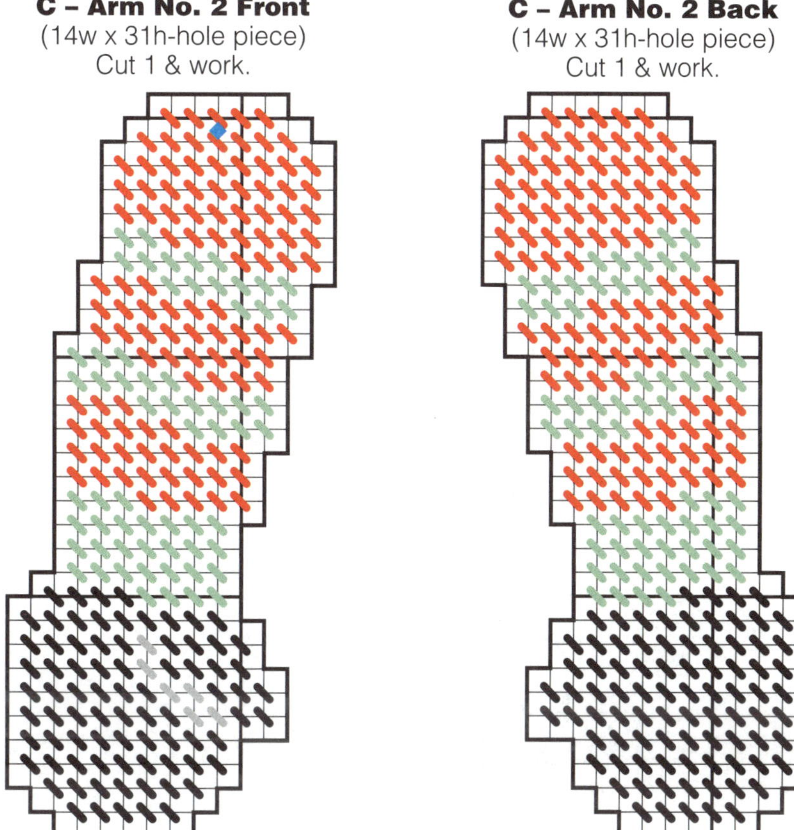

C – Arm No. 2 Front
(14w x 31h-hole piece)
Cut 1 & work.

C – Arm No. 2 Back
(14w x 31h-hole piece)
Cut 1 & work.

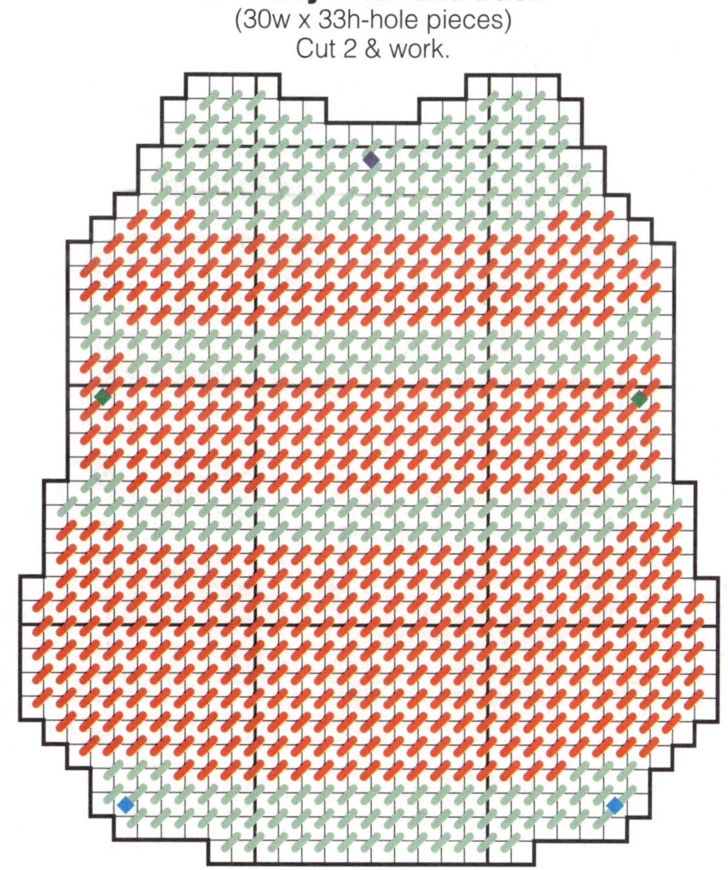

B – Body Front and Back
(30w x 33h-hole pieces)
Cut 2 & work.

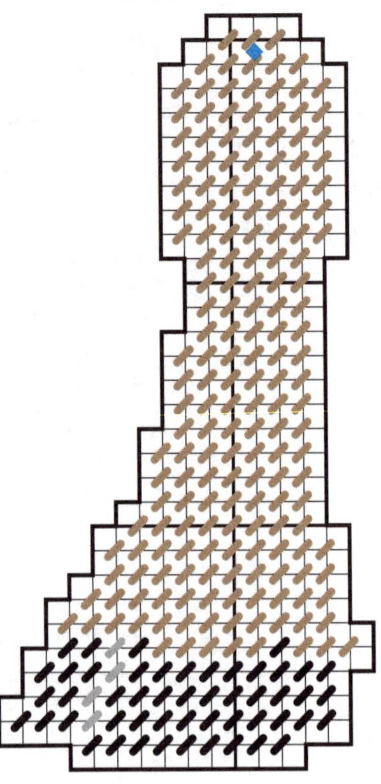

D – Leg Piece No. 1
(16w x 31h-hole pieces)
Cut 2 & work.

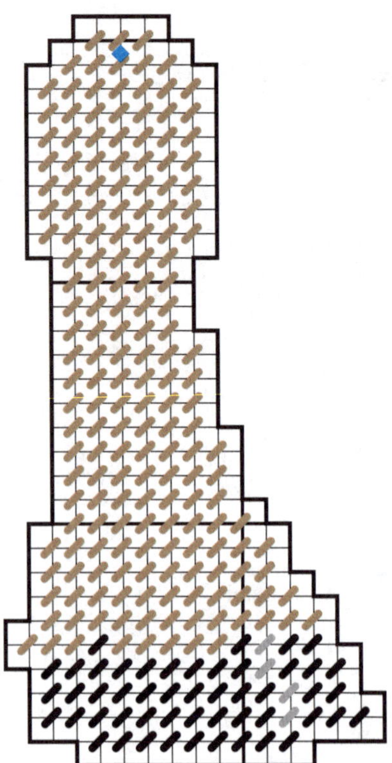

D – Leg Piece No. 2
(16w x 31h-hole pieces)
Cut 2 & work.

Wendy Witch

Size: About 15" x 16" [38.1cm x 40.6cm]
Skill Level: Average

NOTE
• Graphs on pages 5–8.

Stitching Step By Step

1 Cut and work pieces according to graphs. Using black (Separate into individual plies if desired.) and embroidery stitches indicated, embroider detail on Front A and No. 1 Front C as indicated on graphs.

2 With matching colors as shown in photo on back cover, whipstitch A pieces wrong sides together; repeat with B pieces. For Arms (make 2), whipstitch two corresponding C pieces wrong sides together. For Legs (make 2), whipstitch two corresponding D pieces wrong sides together.

3 Matching same-colored ◆s, with matching colors, tack pieces together as indicated. Glue eyes to Head Front as indicated. Hang or display as desired.

Materials

❑ Four sheets of 7-mesh plastic canvas
❑ Two 8mm wiggle eyes
❑ Craft glue or glue gun
❑ Worsted-weight or plastic canvas yarn; for amounts see Color Key.

COLOR KEY
Wendy Witch

WORSTED-WEIGHT		WORSTED-WEIGHT	
Bright Purple	3 oz. [85.1g]	Fern	10 yds. [9.1m]
Black	40 yds. [36.6m]	Brown	4 yds. [3.7m]
Dk. Gray	20 yds. [18.3m]	Yellow	4 yds. [3.7m]
Peach	20 yds. [18.3m]	Flesh Tone	2 yds. [1.8m]
Christmas Red	12 yds. [11m]	White	1/4 yd. [0.2m]

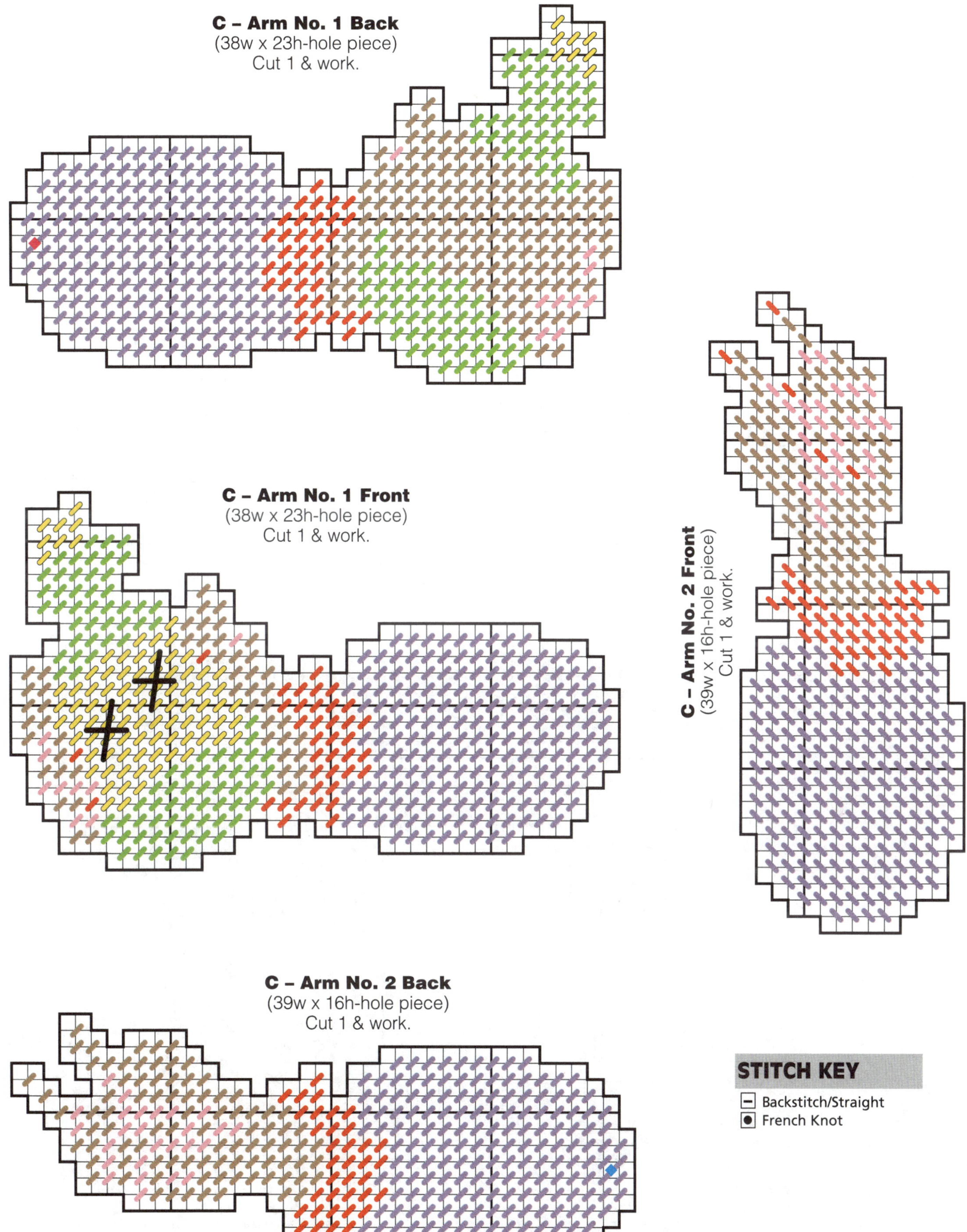

C – Arm No. 1 Back
(38w x 23h-hole piece)
Cut 1 & work.

C – Arm No. 1 Front
(38w x 23h-hole piece)
Cut 1 & work.

C – Arm No. 2 Front
(39w x 16h-hole piece)
Cut 1 & work.

C – Arm No. 2 Back
(39w x 16h-hole piece)
Cut 1 & work.

STITCH KEY
– Backstitch/Straight
● French Knot

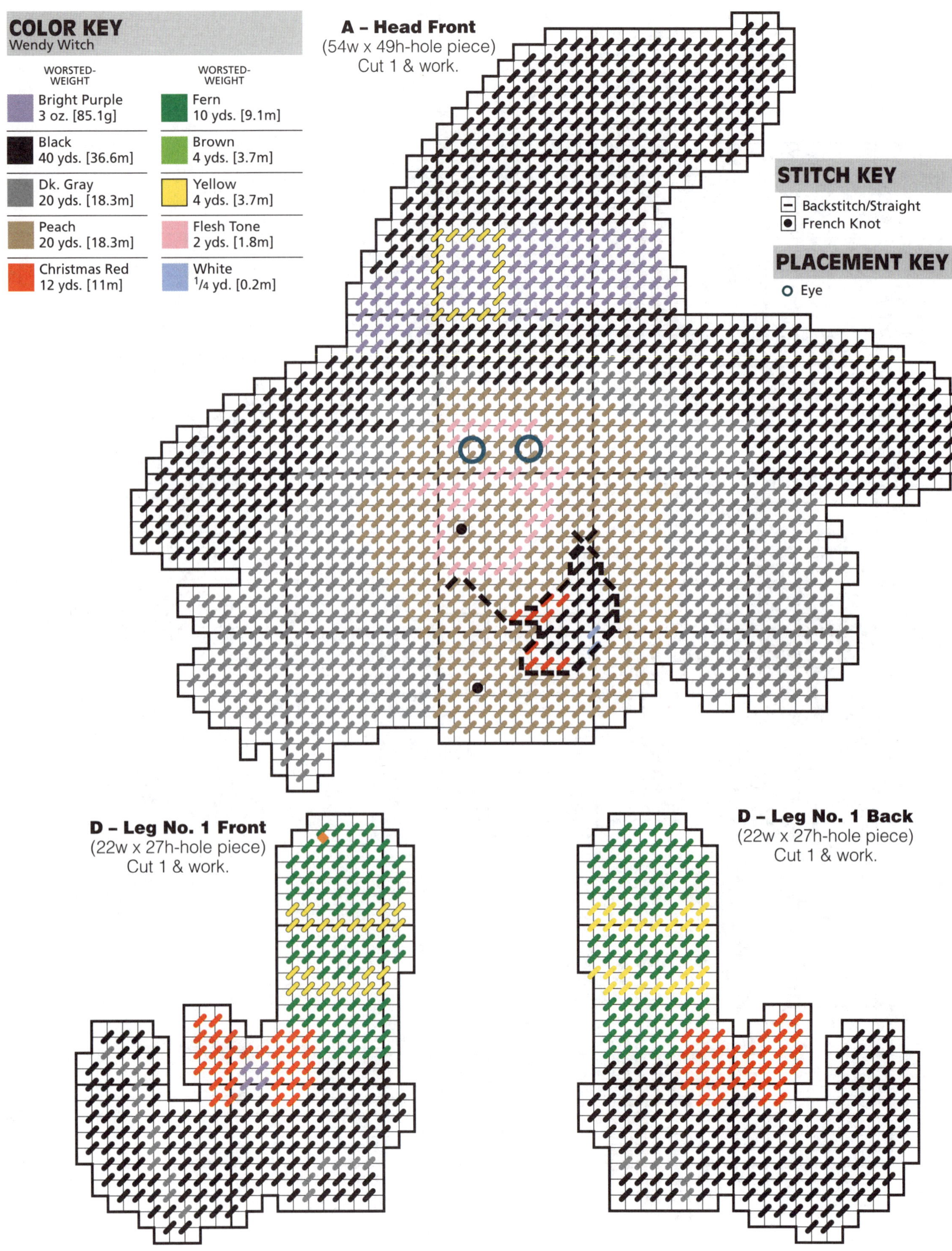

COLOR KEY
Wendy Witch

WORSTED-WEIGHT
Bright Purple
3 oz. [85.1g]
Black
40 yds. [36.6m]
Dk. Gray
20 yds. [18.3m]
Peach
20 yds. [18.3m]
Christmas Red
12 yds. [11m]

WORSTED-WEIGHT
Fern
10 yds. [9.1m]
Brown
4 yds. [3.7m]
Yellow
4 yds. [3.7m]
Flesh Tone
2 yds. [1.8m]
White
1/4 yd. [0.2m]

STITCH KEY
Backstitch/Straight
French Knot

PLACEMENT KEY
Eye

A – Head Front
(54w x 49h-hole piece)
Cut 1 & work.

D – Leg No. 1 Front
(22w x 27h-hole piece)
Cut 1 & work.

D – Leg No. 1 Back
(22w x 27h-hole piece)
Cut 1 & work.

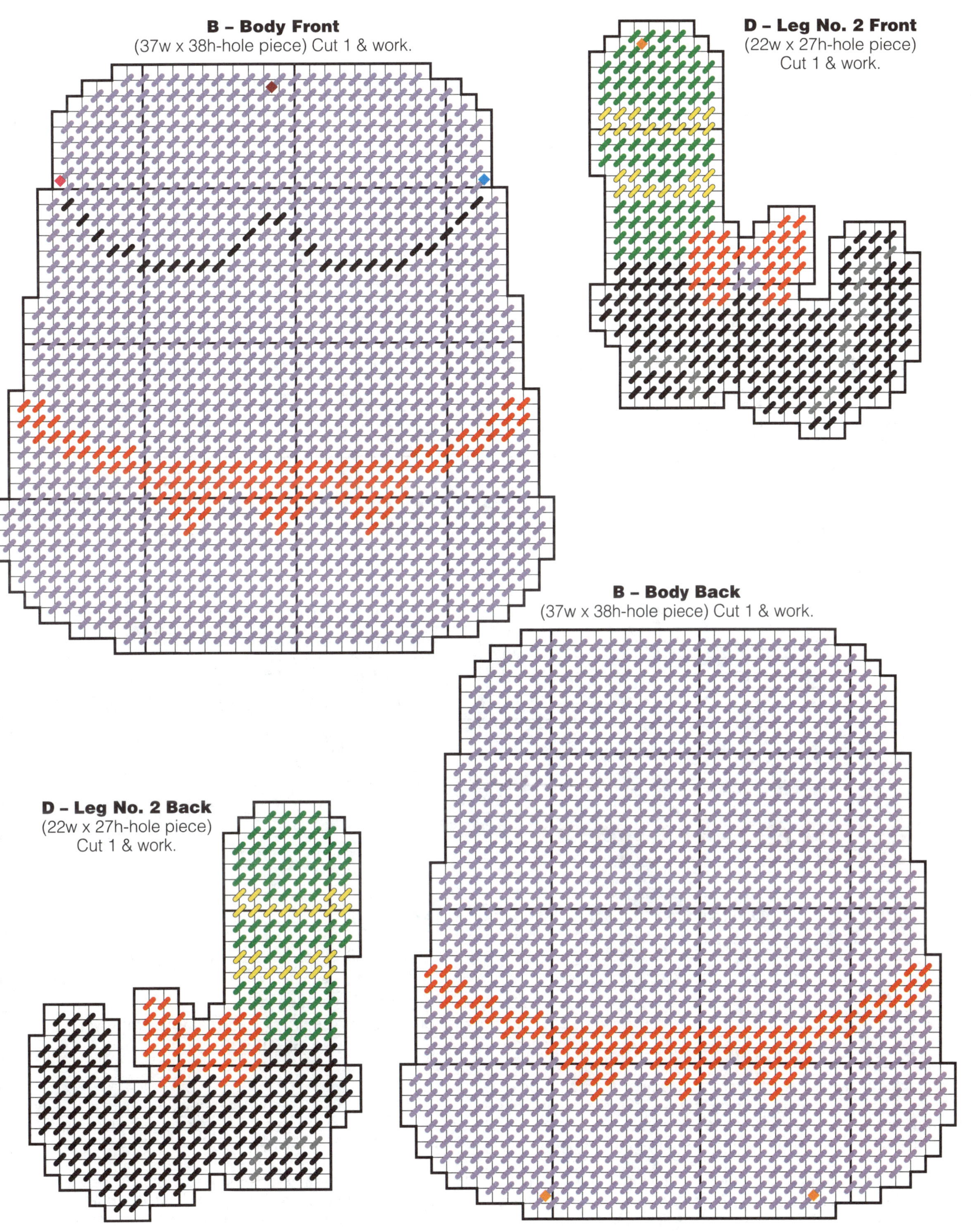

B – Body Front
(37w x 38h-hole piece) Cut 1 & work.

D – Leg No. 2 Front
(22w x 27h-hole piece)
Cut 1 & work.

B – Body Back
(37w x 38h-hole piece) Cut 1 & work.

D – Leg No. 2 Back
(22w x 27h-hole piece)
Cut 1 & work.

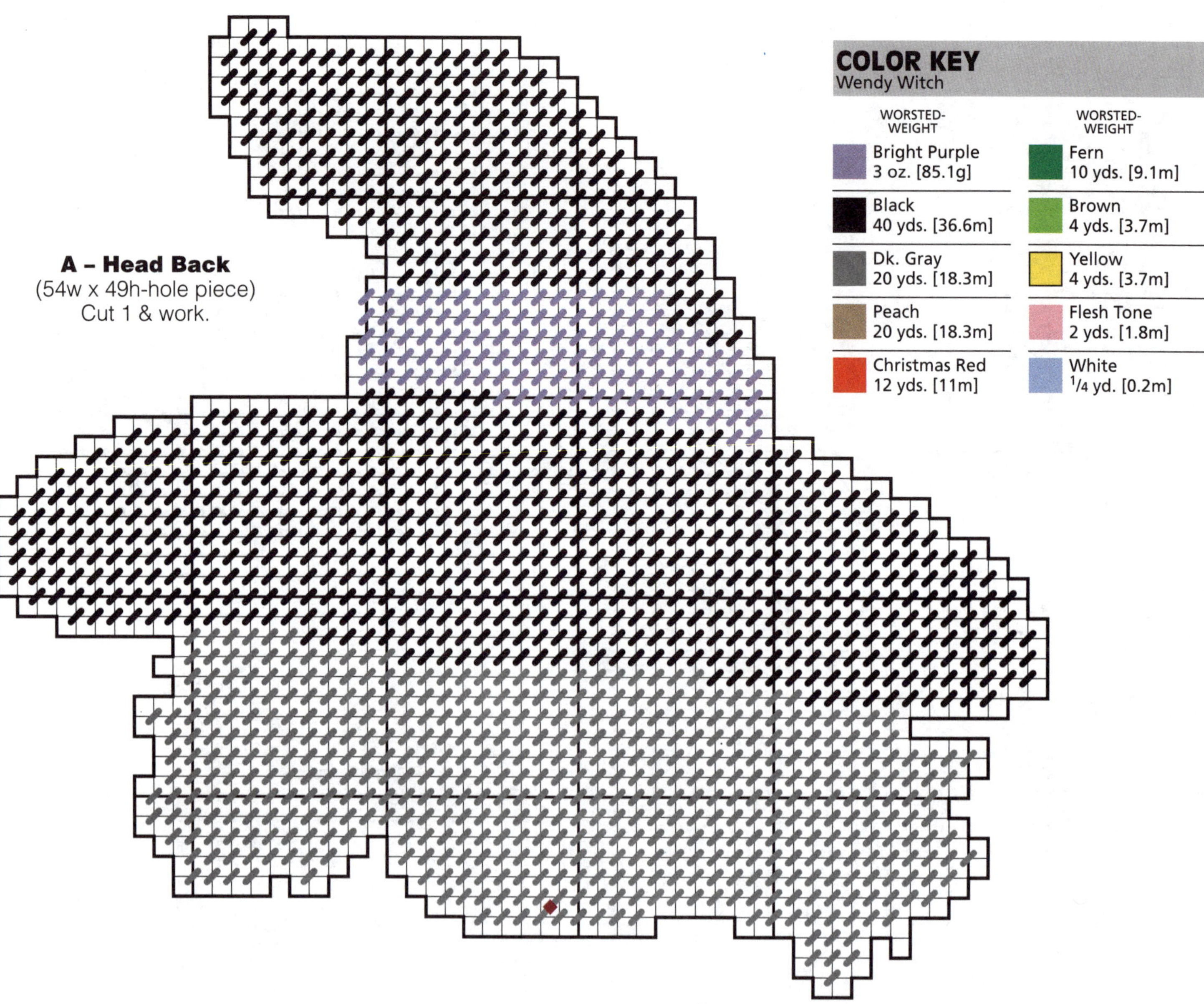

Easter Bunny

Size: About 12" x 15" [30.5cm x 38.1cm]
Skill Level: Average

NOTE
• Graphs on pages 9 –11.

Stitching Step By Step

1 Cut and work pieces according to graphs. Using dk. brown (Separate into individual plies if desired.) and embroidery stitches indicated, embroider detail on Front A and Front B as indicated on graphs.

2 With matching colors as shown in photo on back cover, whipstitch A pieces wrong sides together; repeat with B pieces. For Arms (make 2), whipstitch two corresponding C pieces wrong sides together. For Legs (make 2), whipstitch two corresponding D pieces wrong sides together.

3 Matching same-colored ◆s, with matching colors, tack pieces together as indicated. Glue eyes to Head Front as indicated. Hang or display as desired.

Materials

❑ Three sheets of 7-mesh plastic canvas
❑ Two 8mm wiggle eyes
❑ Craft glue or glue gun
❑ Worsted-weight or plastic canvas yarn; for amounts see Color Key.

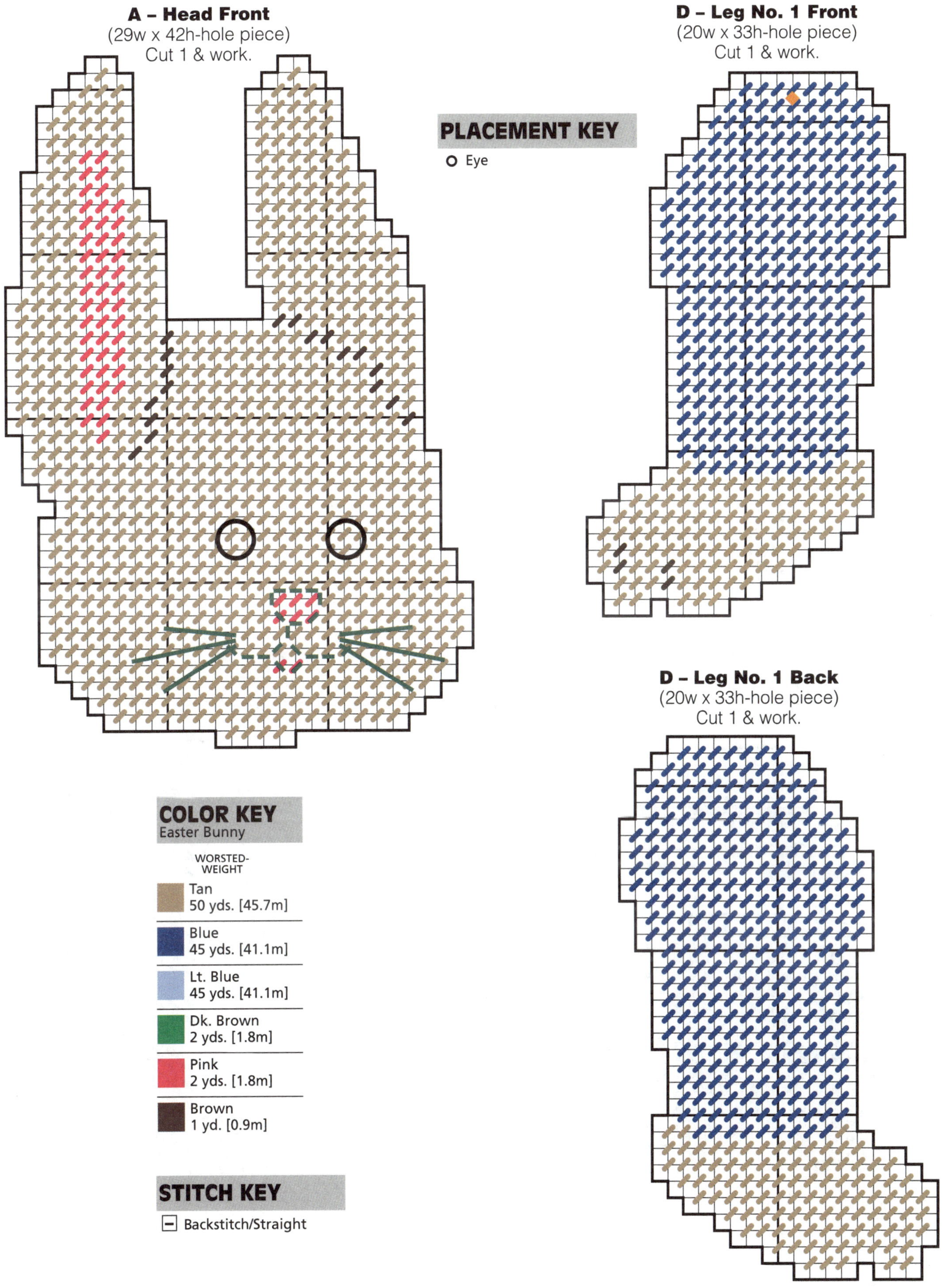

A – Head Front
(29w x 42h-hole piece)
Cut 1 & work.

D – Leg No. 1 Front
(20w x 33h-hole piece)
Cut 1 & work.

PLACEMENT KEY
O Eye

D – Leg No. 1 Back
(20w x 33h-hole piece)
Cut 1 & work.

COLOR KEY
Easter Bunny

WORSTED-WEIGHT
Tan
50 yds. [45.7m]

Blue
45 yds. [41.1m]

Lt. Blue
45 yds. [41.1m]

Dk. Brown
2 yds. [1.8m]

Pink
2 yds. [1.8m]

Brown
1 yd. [0.9m]

STITCH KEY
☐ Backstitch/Straight

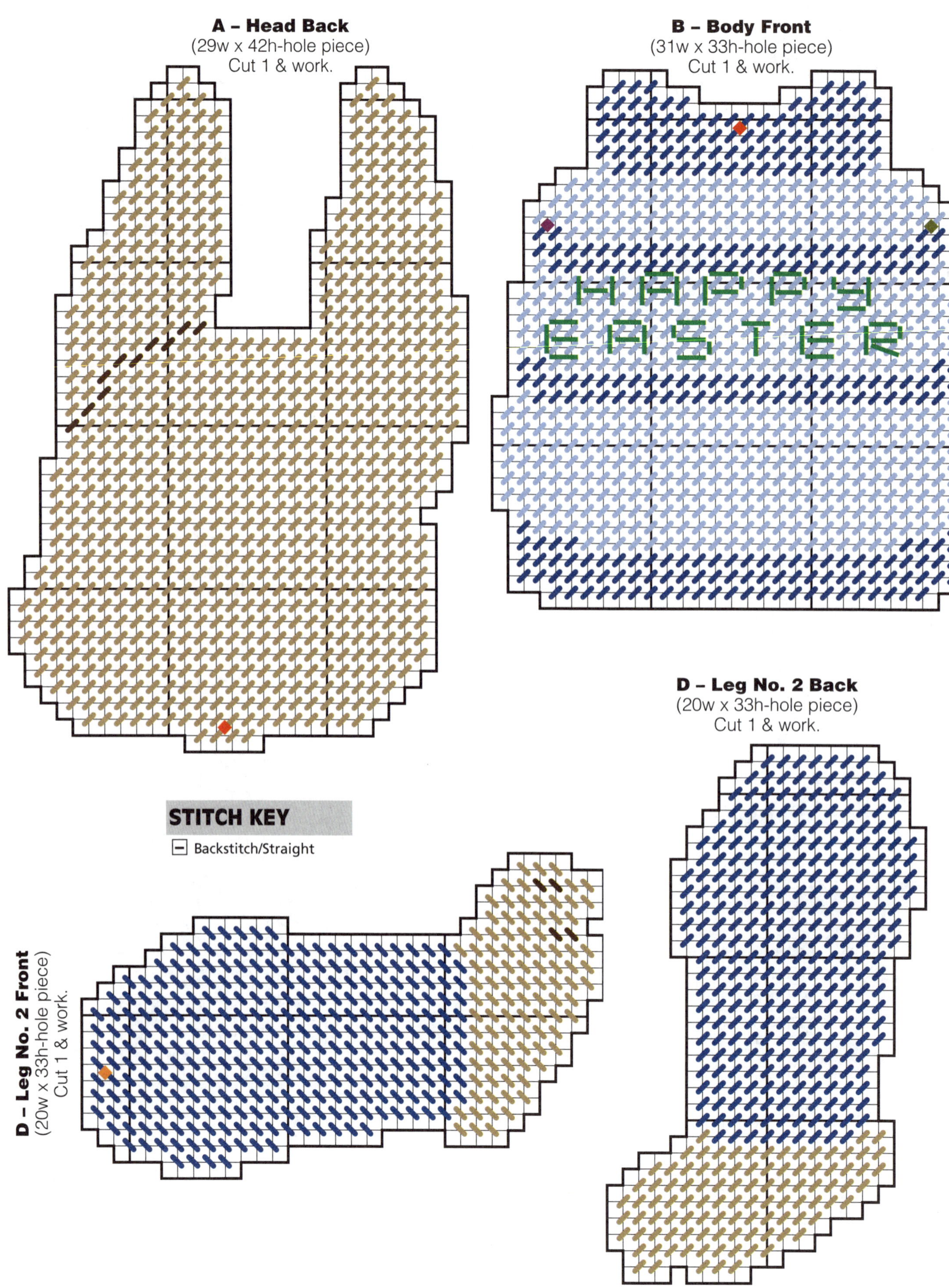

A – Head Back
(29w x 42h-hole piece)
Cut 1 & work.

B – Body Front
(31w x 33h-hole piece)
Cut 1 & work.

HAPPY EASTER

D – Leg No. 2 Back
(20w x 33h-hole piece)
Cut 1 & work.

STITCH KEY
Backstitch/Straight

D – Leg No. 2 Front
(20w x 33h-hole piece)
Cut 1 & work.

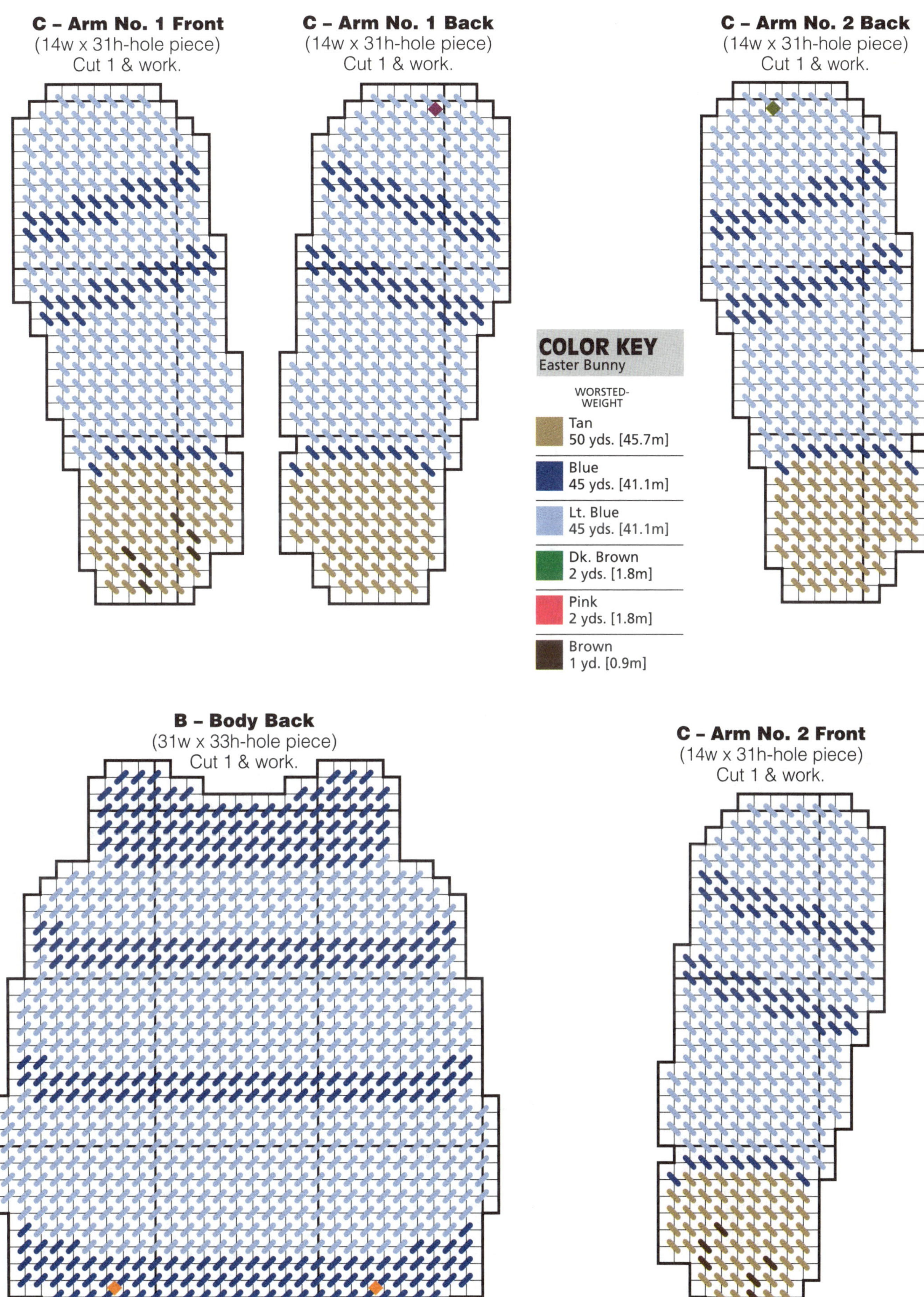
C – Arm No. 1 Front
(14w x 31h-hole piece)
Cut 1 & work.

C – Arm No. 1 Back
(14w x 31h-hole piece)
Cut 1 & work.

C – Arm No. 2 Back
(14w x 31h-hole piece)
Cut 1 & work.

COLOR KEY
Easter Bunny
WORSTED-WEIGHT
Tan
50 yds. [45.7m]
Blue
45 yds. [41.1m]
Lt. Blue
45 yds. [41.1m]
Dk. Brown
2 yds. [1.8m]
Pink
2 yds. [1.8m]
Brown
1 yd. [0.9m]

B – Body Back
(31w x 33h-hole piece)
Cut 1 & work.

C – Arm No. 2 Front
(14w x 31h-hole piece)
Cut 1 & work.

Uncle Sam

Size: About 14¾" x 14½" [37.5cm x 36.8cm]
Skill Level: Average

NOTE
- Graphs continued on pages 13 and 14.

Stitching Step By Step

1 Cut and work pieces according to graphs. Using colors (Separate into individual plies if desired.) and embroidery stitches indicated, embroider detail on Front A and Front B as indicated on graphs.

2 With matching colors as shown in photo on back cover, whipstitch A pieces wrong sides together; repeat with B pieces. For Arms (make 2), whipstitch two corresponding C pieces wrong sides together. For Legs (make 2), whipstitch one D No. 1 and one D No. 2 wrong sides together.

3 Matching same-colored ◆s, with matching colors, tack pieces together as indicated. Glue eyes to Head Front as indicated. Hang or display as desired.

Materials
- Three sheets of 7-mesh plastic canvas
- Two 8mm wiggle eyes
- Craft glue or glue gun
- Metallic craft cord; for amount see Color Key.
- Worsted-weight or plastic canvas yarn; for amounts see Color Key.

STITCH KEY
- − Backstitch/Straight
- ● French Knot

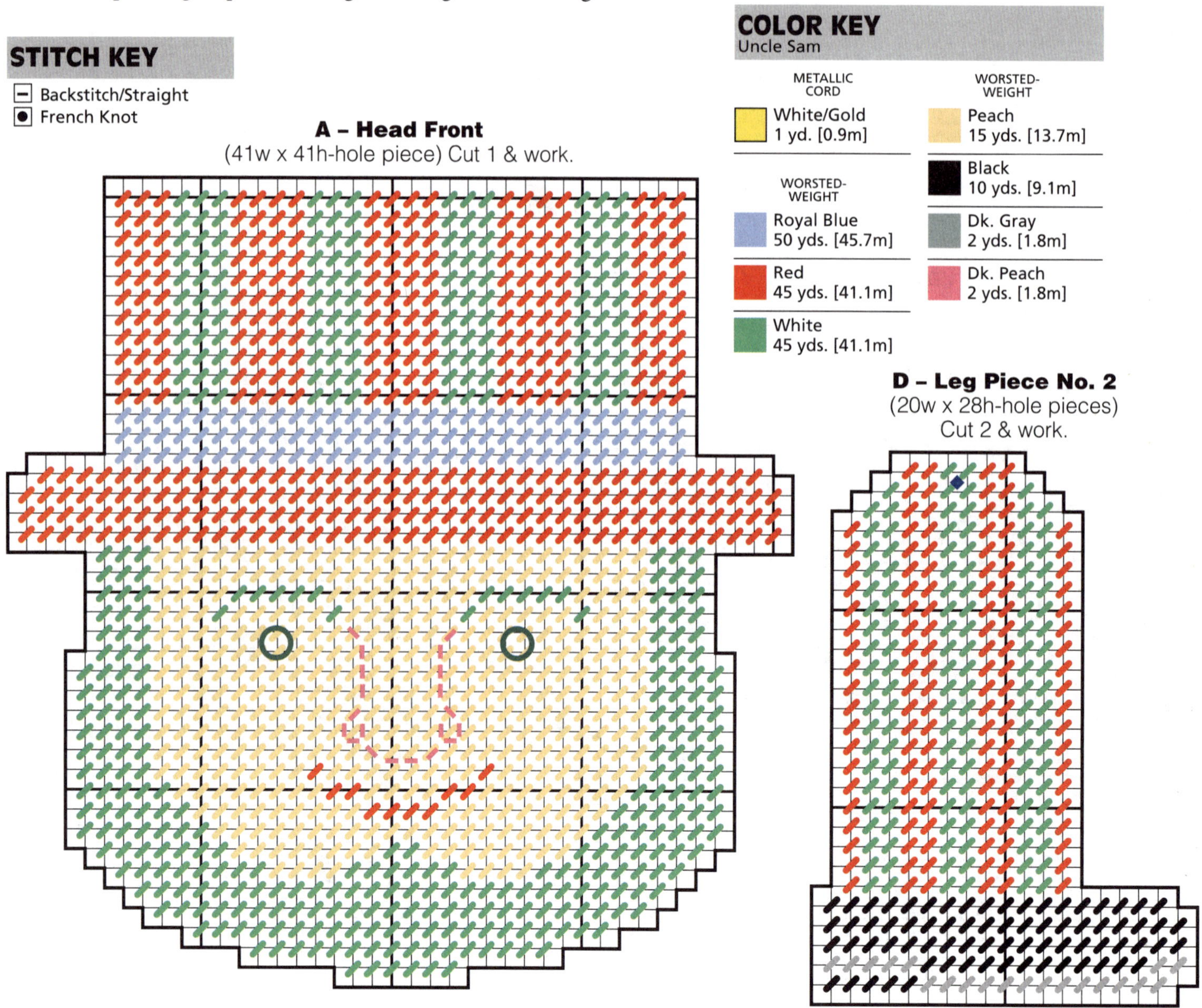

COLOR KEY
Uncle Sam

METALLIC CORD		WORSTED-WEIGHT	
White/Gold	1 yd. [0.9m]	Peach	15 yds. [13.7m]

WORSTED-WEIGHT			
Royal Blue	50 yds. [45.7m]	Black	10 yds. [9.1m]
Red	45 yds. [41.1m]	Dk. Gray	2 yds. [1.8m]
White	45 yds. [41.1m]	Dk. Peach	2 yds. [1.8m]

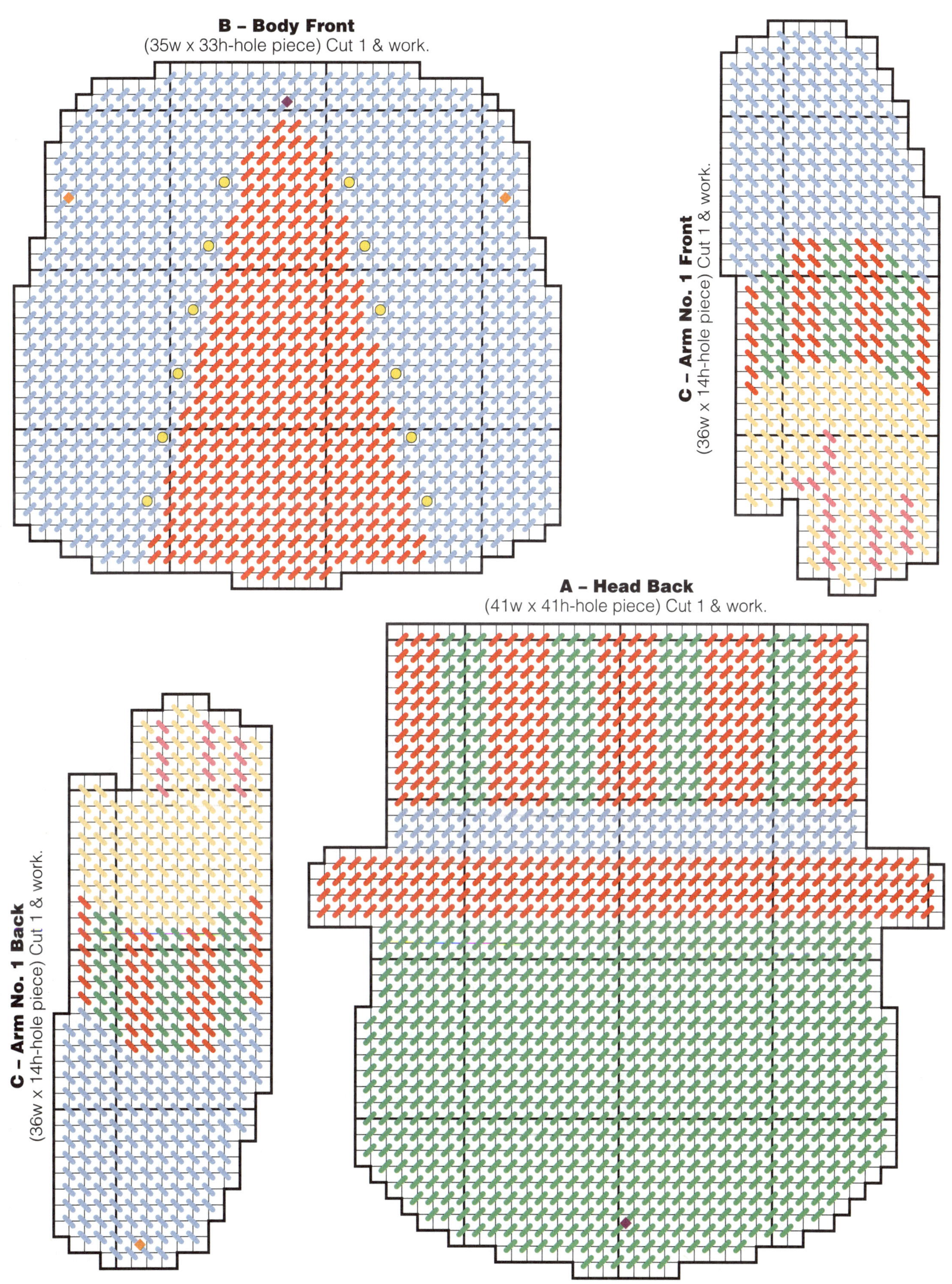

B – Body Front
(35w x 33h-hole piece) Cut 1 & work.
C – Arm No. 1 Front
(36w x 14h-hole piece) Cut 1 & work.
A – Head Back
(41w x 41h-hole piece) Cut 1 & work.
C – Arm No. 1 Back
(36w x 14h-hole piece) Cut 1 & work.

C – Arm No. 2 Front
(36w x 14h-hole piece) Cut 1 & work.

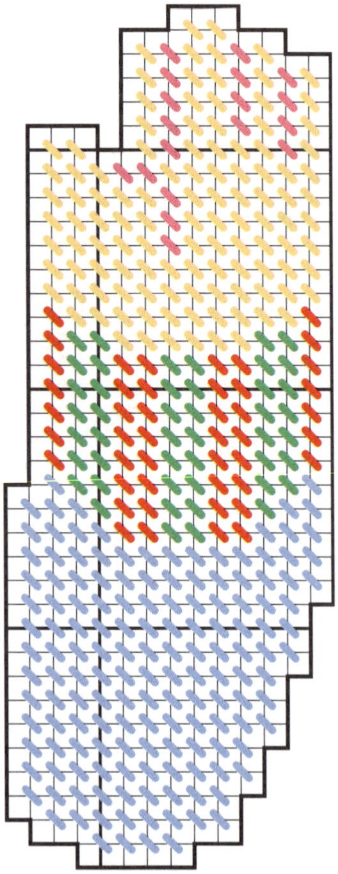

C – Arm No. 2 Back
(36w x 14h-hole piece) Cut 1 & work.

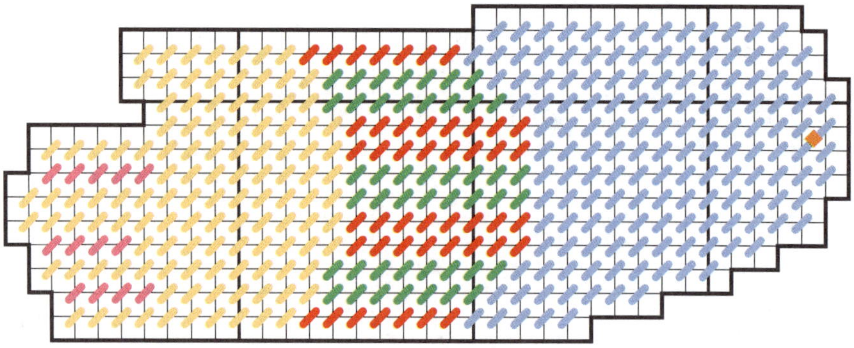

COLOR KEY
Uncle Sam

METALLIC CORD	**WORSTED-WEIGHT**
White/Gold 1 yd. [0.9m]	Peach 15 yds. [13.7m]
WORSTED-WEIGHT	Black 10 yds. [9.1m]
Royal Blue 50 yds. [45.7m]	Dk. Gray 2 yds. [1.8m]
Red 45 yds. [41.1m]	Dk. Peach 2 yds. [1.8m]
White 45 yds. [41.1m]	

B – Body Back
(35w x 33h-hole piece) Cut 1 & work.

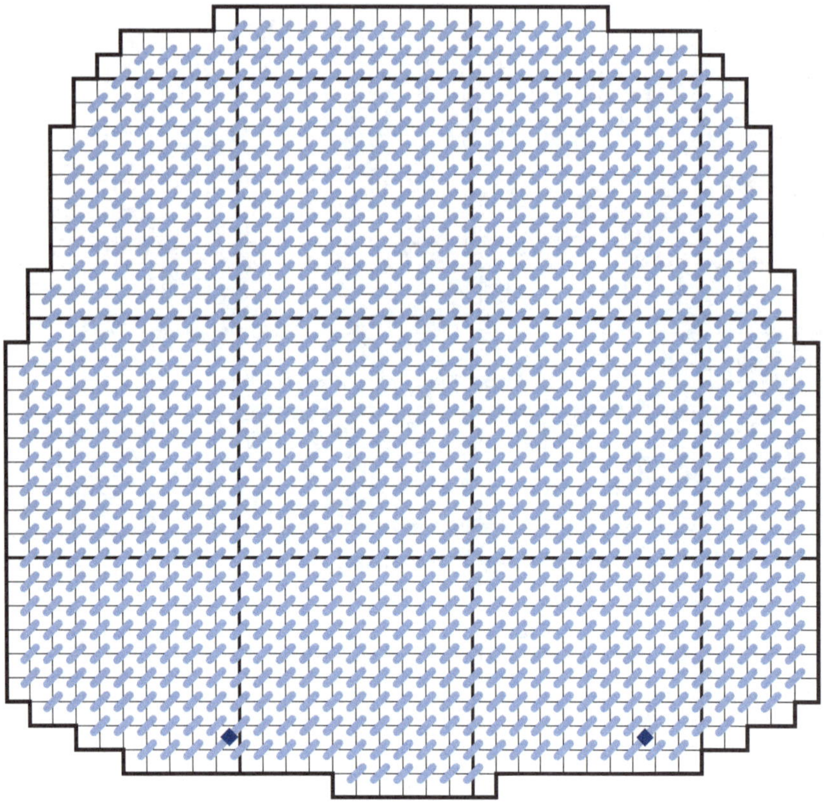

D – Leg Piece No. 1
(20w x 28h-hole pieces)
Cut 2 & work.

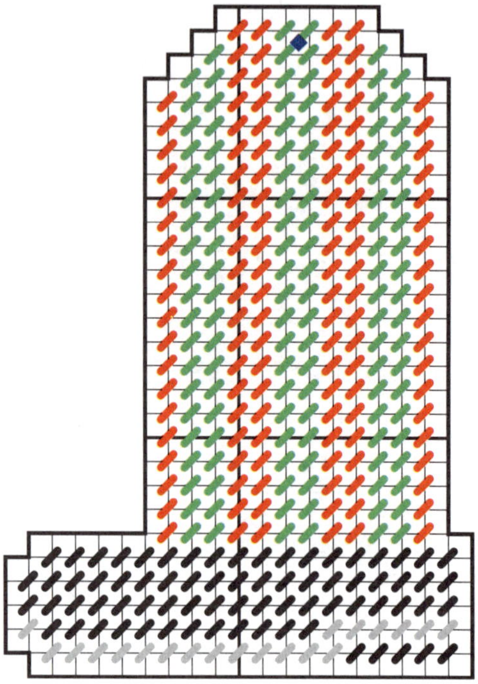

Leprechaun

Size: About 11¾" x 14½" [29.8cm x 36.8cm]
Skill Level: Average

NOTE
- Graphs continued on pages 16–18.

Stitching Step By Step

1 Cut and work pieces according to graphs. Using colors (Separate into individual plies if desired.) and embroidery stitches indicated, embroider detail on Front A and Front B as indicated on graphs.

2 With matching colors as shown in photo on back cover, whipstitch A pieces wrong sides together; repeat with B pieces. For Arms (make 2), whipstitch two corresponding C pieces wrong sides together. For Legs (make 2), whipstitch two corresponding D pieces wrong sides together.

3 Matching same-colored ◆s, with matching colors, tack pieces together as indicated. Glue eyes to Head Front as indicated. Hang or display as desired.

Materials
- Three sheets of 7-mesh plastic canvas
- Two 8mm wiggle eyes
- Craft glue or glue gun
- Metallic craft cord; for amount see Color Key.
- Worsted-weight or plastic canvas yarn; for amounts see Color Key.

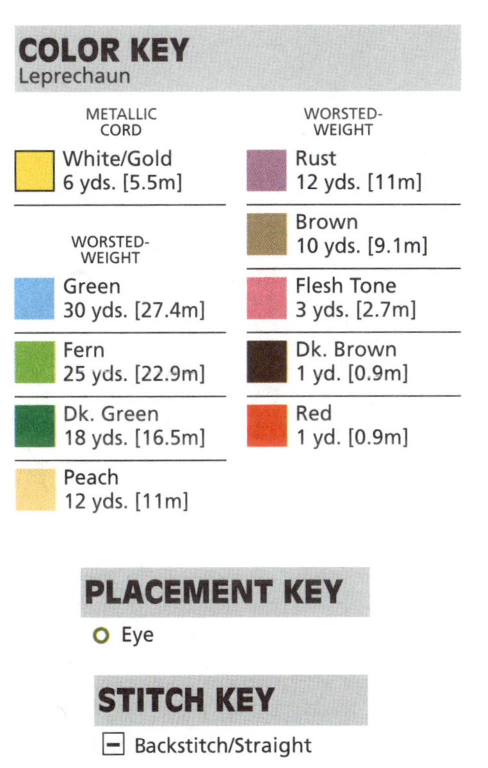

COLOR KEY
Leprechaun

METALLIC CORD		WORSTED-WEIGHT	
White/Gold	6 yds. [5.5m]	Rust	12 yds. [11m]

WORSTED-WEIGHT			
Green	30 yds. [27.4m]	Brown	10 yds. [9.1m]
Fern	25 yds. [22.9m]	Flesh Tone	3 yds. [2.7m]
Dk. Green	18 yds. [16.5m]	Dk. Brown	1 yd. [0.9m]
Peach	12 yds. [11m]	Red	1 yd. [0.9m]

PLACEMENT KEY
- ○ Eye

STITCH KEY
- ⊟ Backstitch/Straight

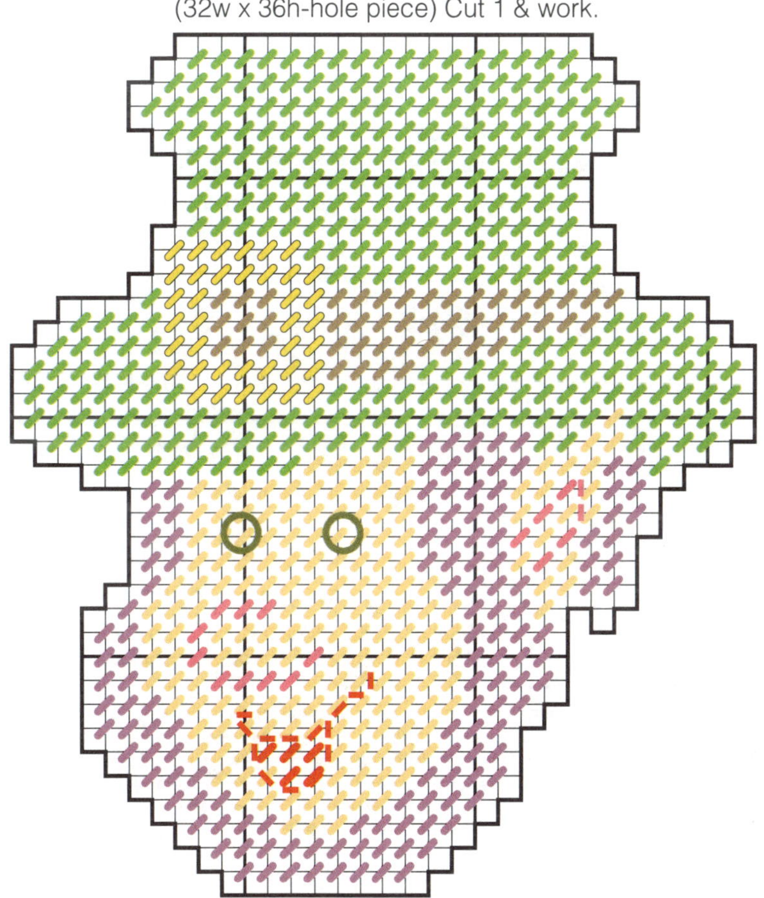

A – Head Front
(32w x 36h-hole piece) Cut 1 & work.

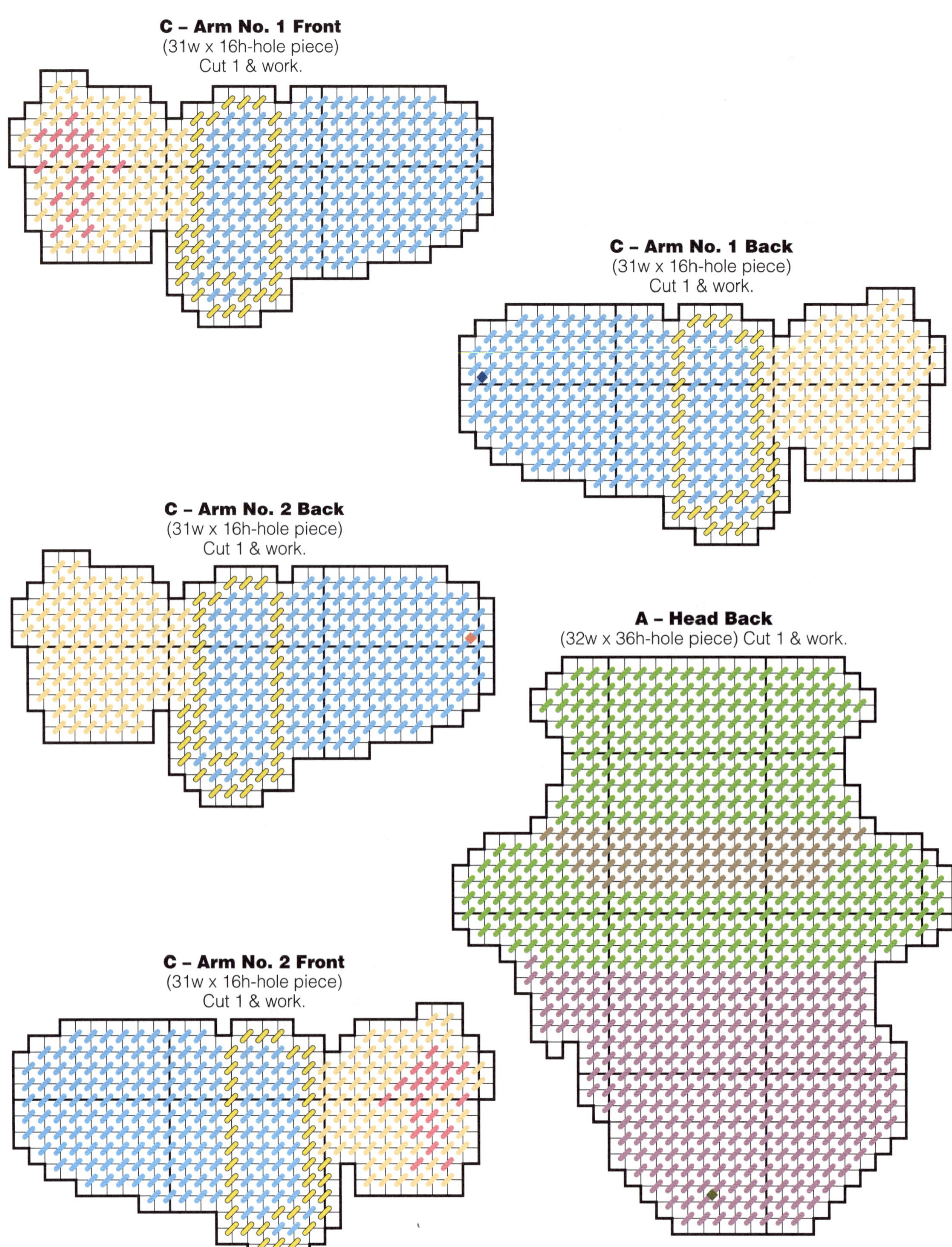

C – Arm No. 1 Front
(31w x 16h-hole piece)
Cut 1 & work.

C – Arm No. 1 Back
(31w x 16h-hole piece)
Cut 1 & work.

C – Arm No. 2 Back
(31w x 16h-hole piece)
Cut 1 & work.

A – Head Back
(32w x 36h-hole piece) Cut 1 & work.

C – Arm No. 2 Front
(31w x 16h-hole piece)
Cut 1 & work.

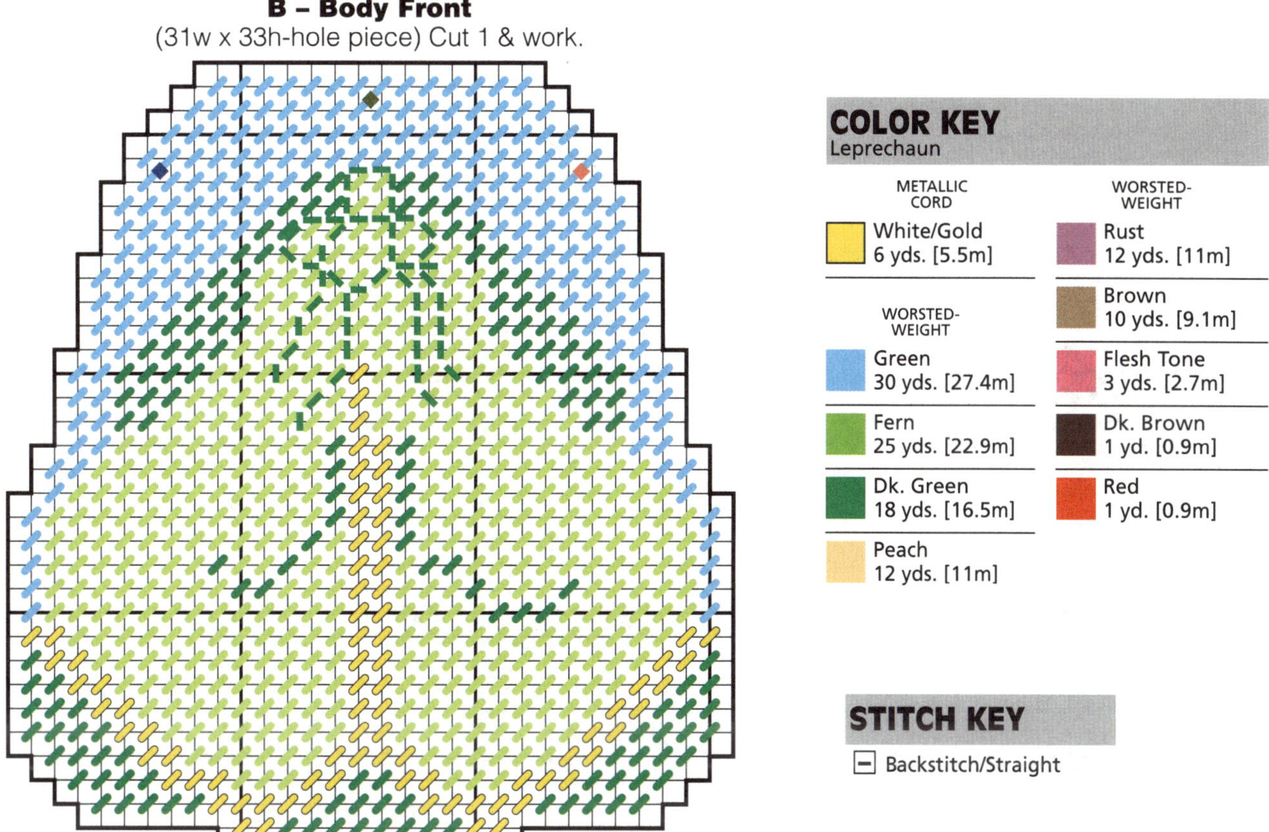

B – Body Front

(31w x 33h-hole piece) Cut 1 & work.

COLOR KEY
Leprechaun

METALLIC CORD
- White/Gold 6 yds. [5.5m]

WORSTED-WEIGHT
- Green 30 yds. [27.4m]
- Fern 25 yds. [22.9m]
- Dk. Green 18 yds. [16.5m]
- Peach 12 yds. [11m]

WORSTED-WEIGHT
- Rust 12 yds. [11m]
- Brown 10 yds. [9.1m]
- Flesh Tone 3 yds. [2.7m]
- Dk. Brown 1 yd. [0.9m]
- Red 1 yd. [0.9m]

STITCH KEY
- Backstitch/Straight

D – Leg No. 1 Back

(17w x 32h-hole piece) Cut 1 & work.

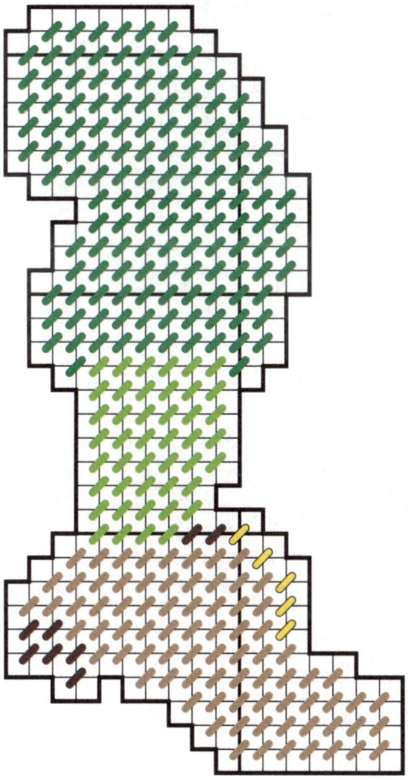

B – Body Back

(31w x 33h-hole piece) Cut 1 & work.

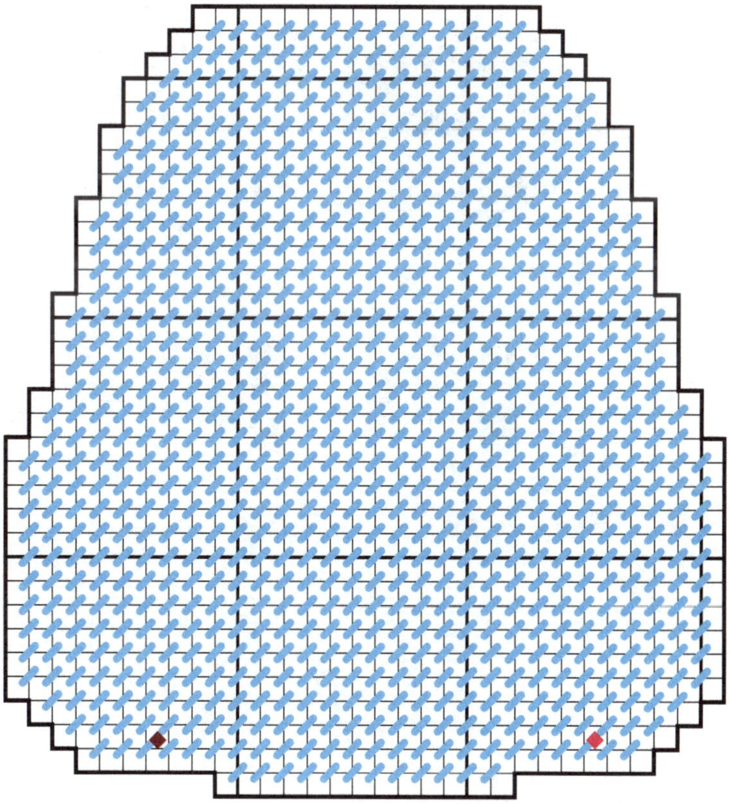

D – Leg No. 2 Back
(17w x 32h-hole piece)
Cut 1 & work.

D – Leg No. 2 Front
(17w x 32h-hole piece)
Cut 1 & work.

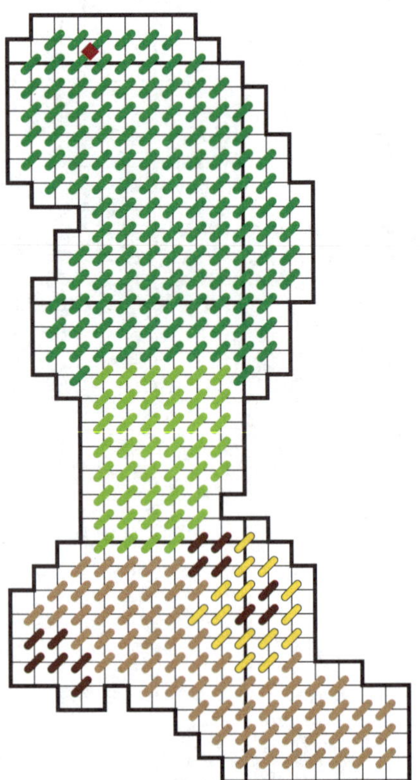

D – Leg No. 1 Front
(17w x 32h-hole piece)
Cut 1 & work.

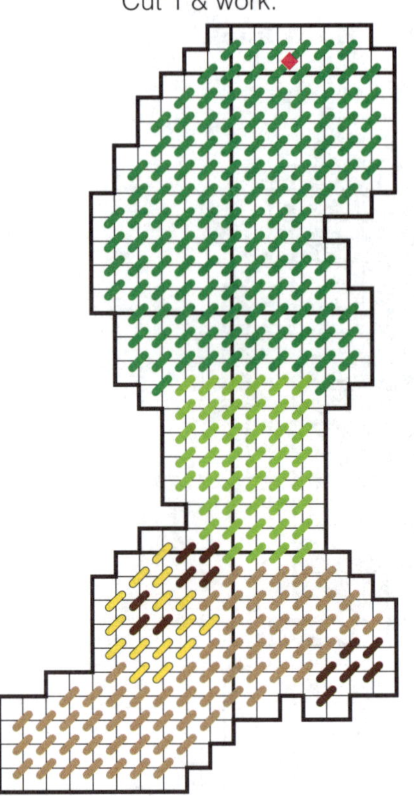

COLOR KEY
Leprechaun

METALLIC CORD

- White/Gold — 6 yds. [5.5m]

WORSTED-WEIGHT

- Green — 30 yds. [27.4m]
- Fern — 25 yds. [22.9m]
- Dk. Green — 18 yds. [16.5m]
- Peach — 12 yds. [11m]
- Rust — 12 yds. [11m]
- Brown — 10 yds. [9.1m]
- Flesh Tone — 3 yds. [2.7m]
- Dk. Brown — 1 yd. [0.9m]
- Red — 1 yd. [0.9m]

Turkey

Size: About 13½" x 13½" [34.3cm x 34.3cm]
Skill Level: Average

NOTE
• Graphs continued on pages 20–22.

Stitching Step By Step

1 Cut and work pieces according to graphs. Using colors (Separate into individual plies if desired.) and embroidery stitches indicated, embroider detail on A and C pieces as indicated on graphs.

2 With matching colors, overcast edges of A and B pieces. For Legs (make 2), whipstitch one C No. 1 and one C No. 2 wrong sides together. With matching colors, whipstitch D pieces wrong sides together.

Materials

❏ Three sheets of 7-mesh plastic canvas
❏ Two 8mm wiggle eyes
❏ Craft glue or glue gun
❏ Worsted-weight or plastic canvas yarn; for amounts see Color Key.

3 Matching ◆s, with tan, tack A and C pieces together as indicated. Glue or tack Body, Wings and Feathers together as shown in photo on back cover. Glue eyes to Body as indicated. Hang or display as desired.

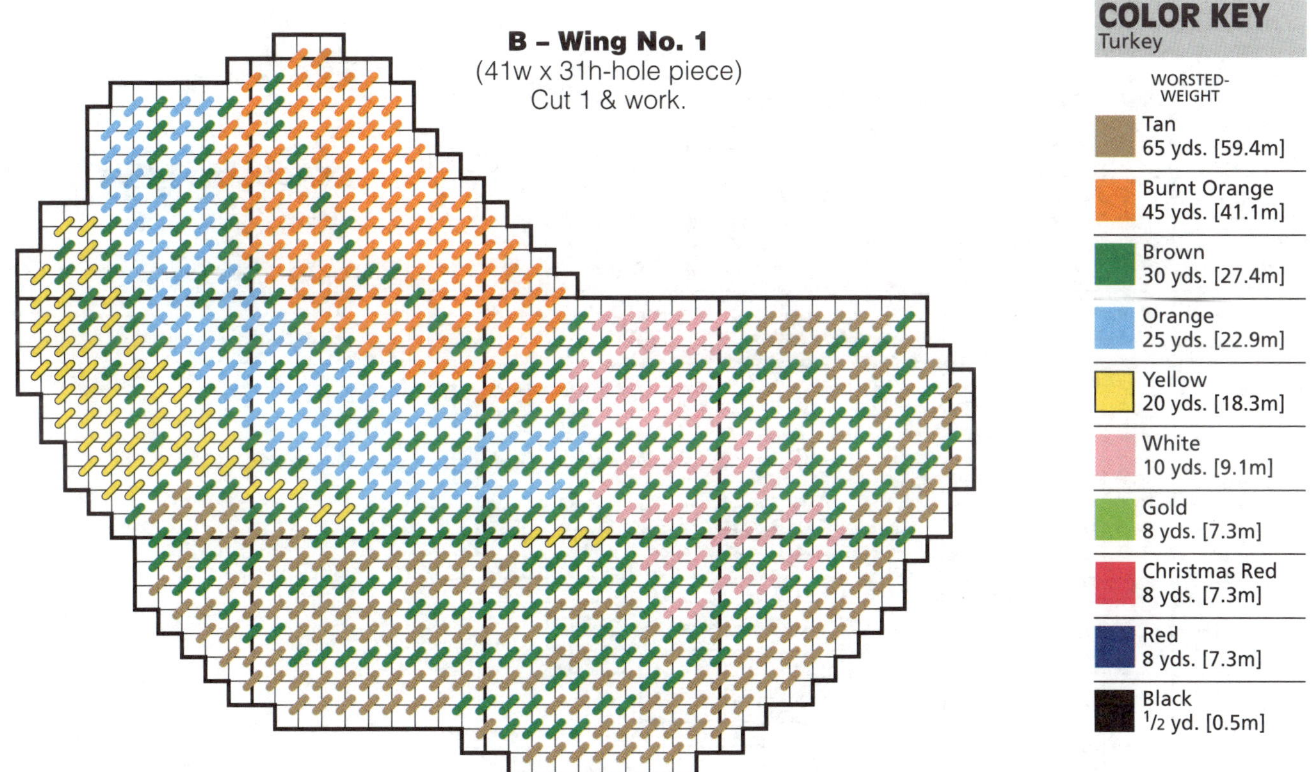

COLOR KEY
Turkey

WORSTED-WEIGHT

Tan	65 yds. [59.4m]
Burnt Orange	45 yds. [41.1m]
Brown	30 yds. [27.4m]
Orange	25 yds. [22.9m]
Yellow	20 yds. [18.3m]
White	10 yds. [9.1m]
Gold	8 yds. [7.3m]
Christmas Red	8 yds. [7.3m]
Red	8 yds. [7.3m]
Black	½ yd. [0.5m]

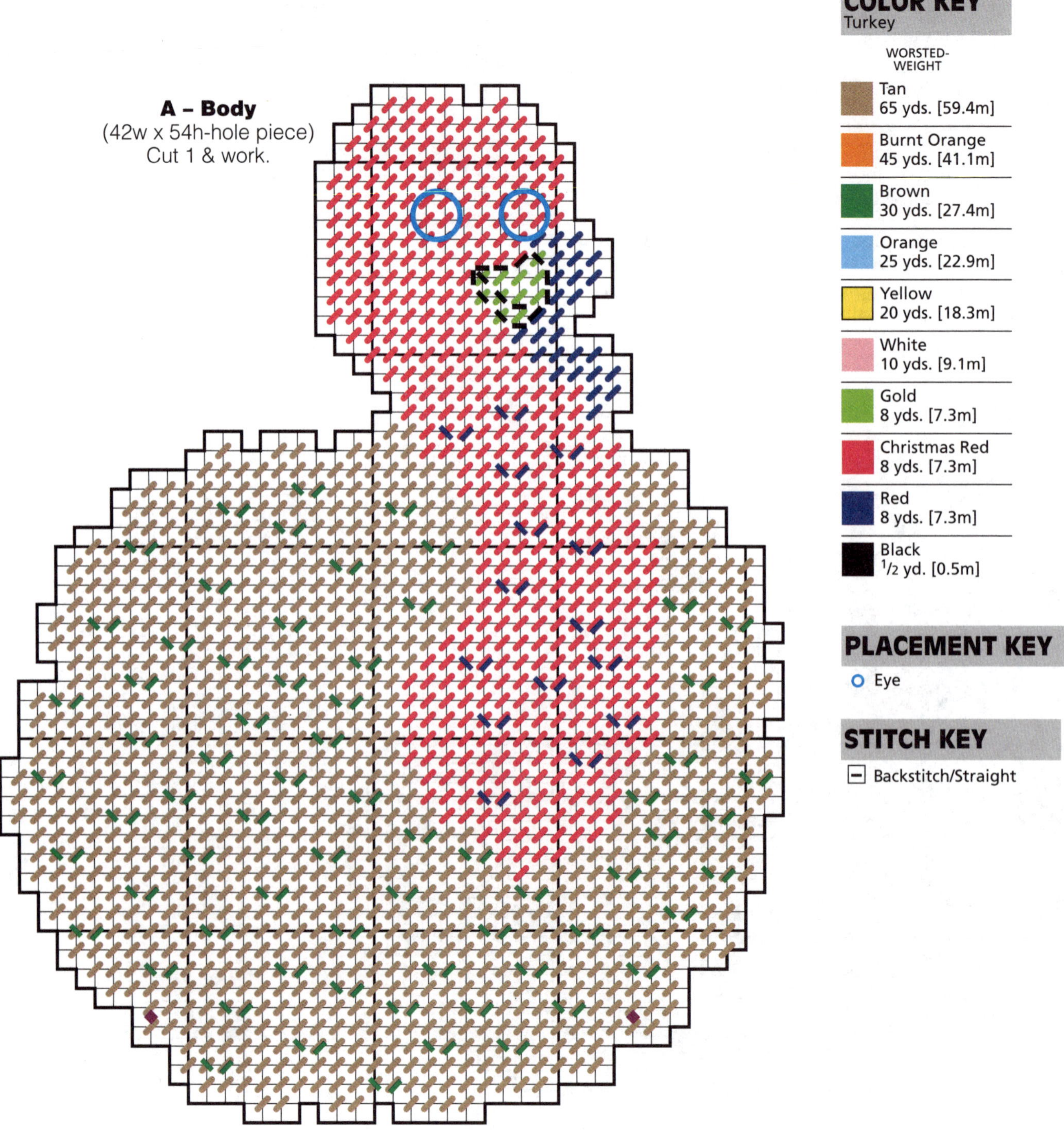

COLOR KEY
Turkey

WORSTED-WEIGHT

	Tan	65 yds. [59.4m]
	Burnt Orange	45 yds. [41.1m]
	Brown	30 yds. [27.4m]
	Orange	25 yds. [22.9m]
	Yellow	20 yds. [18.3m]
	White	10 yds. [9.1m]
	Gold	8 yds. [7.3m]
	Christmas Red	8 yds. [7.3m]
	Red	8 yds. [7.3m]
	Black	1/2 yd. [0.5m]

PLACEMENT KEY

O Eye

STITCH KEY

⊟ Backstitch/Straight

D – Feathers Front and Back

(79w x 48h-hole pieces)
Cut 2 & work.

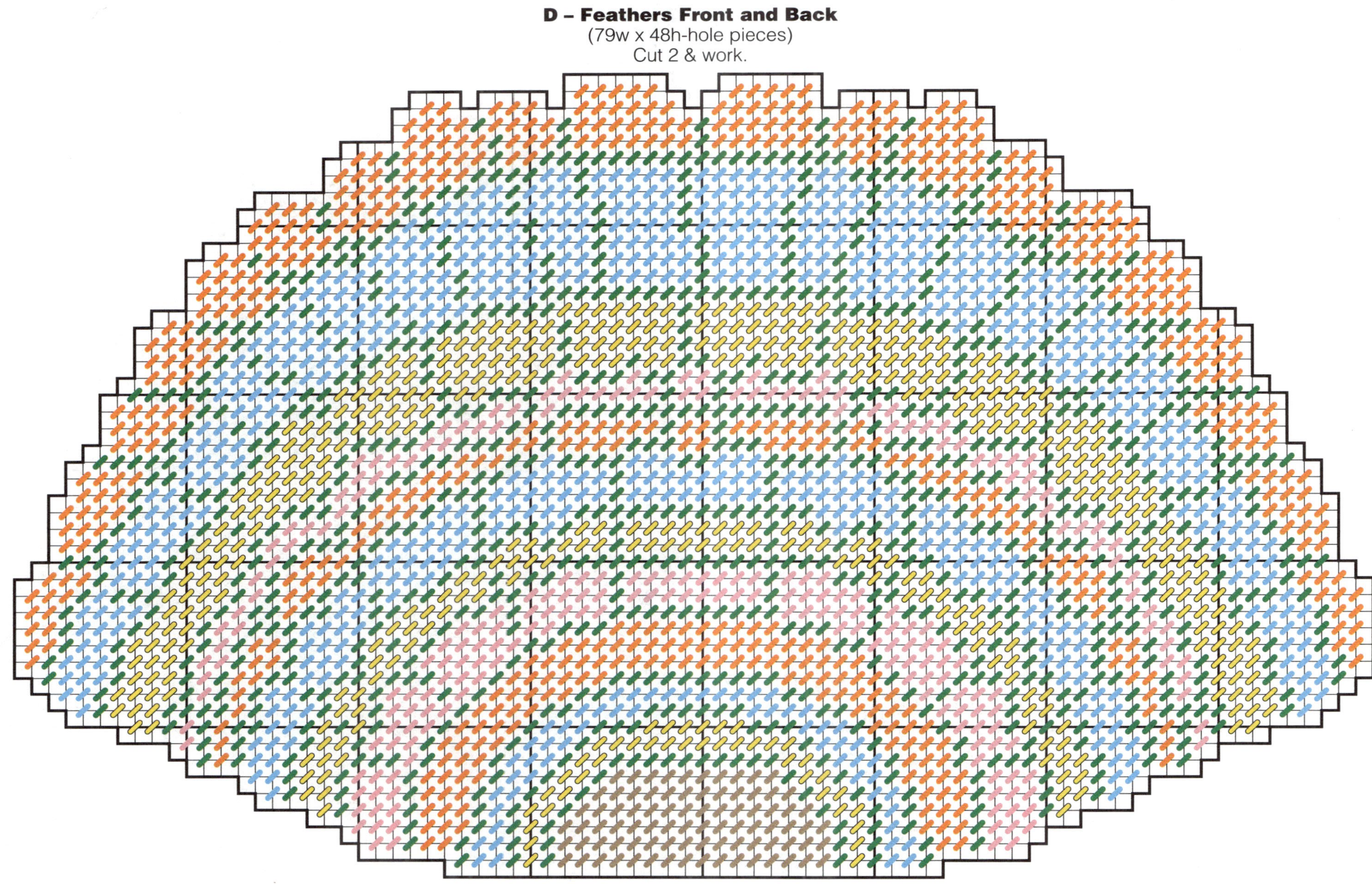

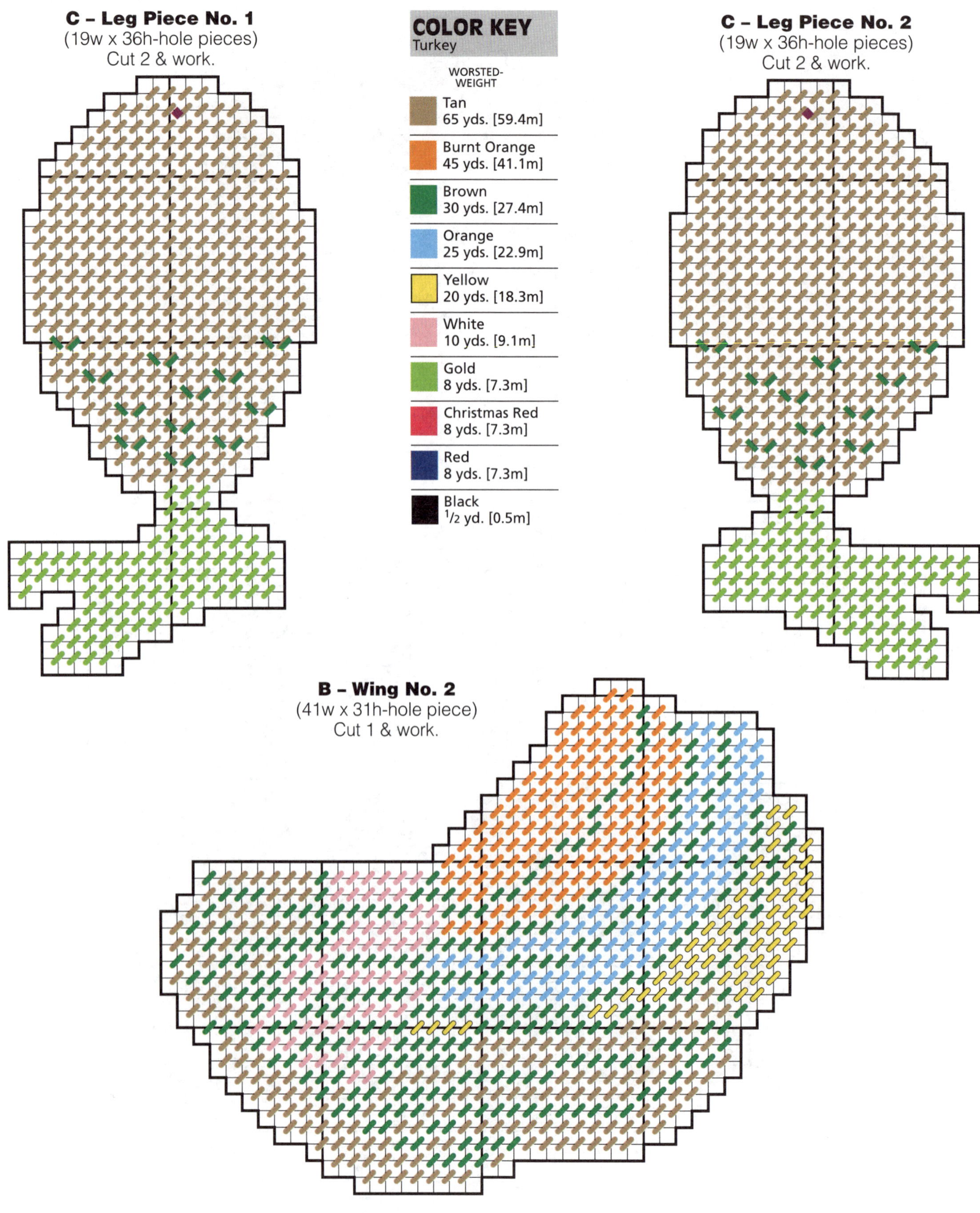

C – Leg Piece No. 1
(19w x 36h-hole pieces)
Cut 2 & work.

C – Leg Piece No. 2
(19w x 36h-hole pieces)
Cut 2 & work.

COLOR KEY
Turkey
WORSTED-WEIGHT
Tan
65 yds. [59.4m]
Burnt Orange
45 yds. [41.1m]
Brown
30 yds. [27.4m]
Orange
25 yds. [22.9m]
Yellow
20 yds. [18.3m]
White
10 yds. [9.1m]
Gold
8 yds. [7.3m]
Christmas Red
8 yds. [7.3m]
Red
8 yds. [7.3m]
Black
1/2 yd. [0.5m]

B – Wing No. 2
(41w x 31h-hole piece)
Cut 1 & work.

23 Old Pecan Road
Big Sandy, TX 75755
www.NeedlecraftShop.com
© 2003 The Needlecraft Shop

The full line of The Needlecraft Shop products is carried by Annie's Attic catalog.

TOLL FREE ORDER LINE
or to request a free catalog
(800) 582-6643
Customer Service
(800) 449-0440
Fax (800) 882-6643
Pattern Services (903) 636-5140
Visit www.AnniesAttic.com

We have made every effort to ensure the accuracy and completeness of these instructions. We cannot, however, be responsible for human error, typographical mistakes or variations in individual work. Reprinting or duplicating the information, photographs or graphics in this publication by any means, including copy machine, computer scanning, digital photography, e-mail, personal Web site and fax, is illegal. Failure to abide by federal copyright laws may result in litigation and fines.

ISBN: 1-57367-142-8

All rights reserved.

Printed in USA

2 3 4 5 6 7 8 9

Shopping for Supplies

For supplies, first shop your local craft and needlework stores. Some supplies may be found in fabric, hardware and discount stores. If you are unable to find the supplies you need, please call (800) 259-4000 for a free catalog that sells plastic canvas supplies.

Before You Cut

Buy one brand of canvas for each entire project, as brands can differ slightly in the distance between bars. Count holes carefully from the graph before you cut, using the bolder lines that show each 10 holes. These 10-mesh lines begin in the lower left-hand corner of each graph to make counting easier. Mark canvas before cutting, then remove all marks completely before stitching. If the piece is cut in a rectangular or square shape and is either not worked, or worked with only one color and one type of stitch, we do not include the graph in the pattern. Instead, we give the cutting and stitching instructions in a separate box.

Covering the Canvas

Bring needle up from back of work, leaving a short length of yarn on back of canvas; work over short length to secure. To end a thread, weave needle and thread through the wrong side of your last few stitches; clip. Follow the numbers on the tiny graphs beside each stitch illustration–bring your needle up from the back of the work on odd numbers and down through the front of the work on even numbers. Work embroidery stitches last, after the canvas has been completely covered by the needlepoint stitches.

Basic Stitches

Continental
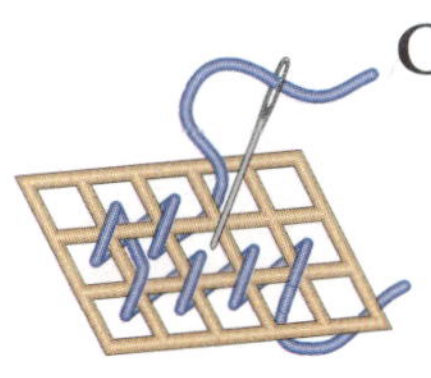

Overcast
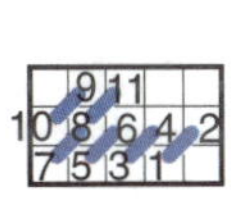

Whipstitch

Slanted Gobelin

Long

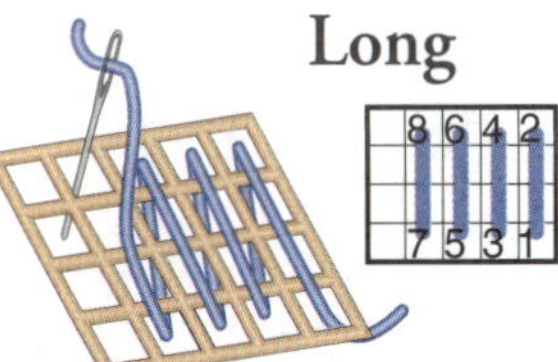

Cross

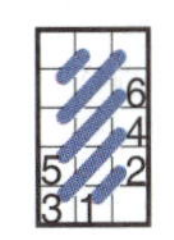

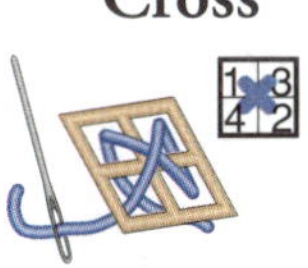

Embroidery Stitches

French Knot
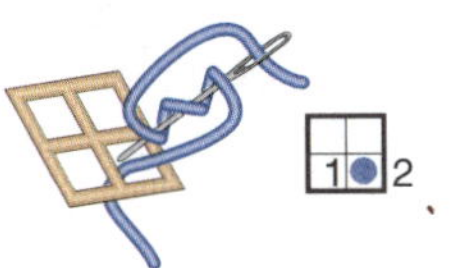

Lazy Daisy
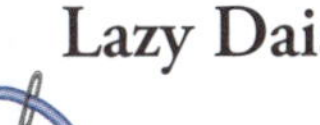
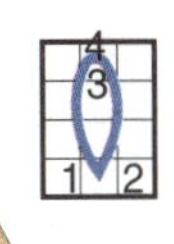

Backstitch
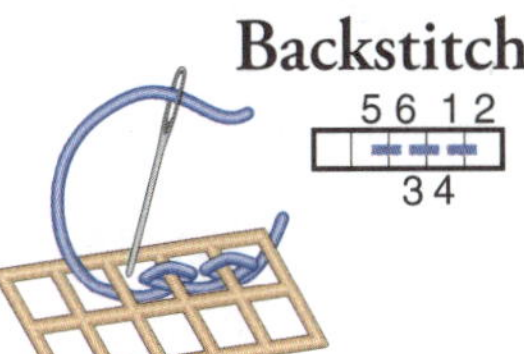

Straight